TOSEL®

READING SERIES

STARTER

READING

2

International TOSEL Committee

CONTENTS

About TOSEL®

TOSEL (Test of Skills in the English Language) was developed to meet the demand for a more effective assessment of English as a foreign language for learners from specific cultural settings.

TOSEL evaluates and certifies the proficiency levels of English learners, from the age of 4 through adulthood, along with academic and job performance results.

Background

- Other English tests are ineffective in accurately measuring individual abilities
- Overuse of US-dominated testing systems in diverse cultural and educational contexts in the global English language learning market

Functions & Usage

- Assessment is categorized into 7 levels
- Used as a qualification for academic excellence for school admissions
- Used as a test to assess the English proficiency in the corporate and public sectors

Goals

- Create an effective tool for assessing and evaluating the English skills of English language learners
- Implement efficient and accessible testing systems and methods
- Provide constructive and developmental English education guidance

TOSEL® Strength

LEVELED ASSESSMENTS

An established English test system fit for seven different levels according to learners' cognitive development

ACCURATE DIAGNOSIS

A systematic and scientific diagnosis of learners' English proficiency

EXTENSIVE MATERIALS

Supplementary materials to help learners in an EFL environment to prepare for TOSEL and improve their proficiency

SUFFICIENT DATA

Content for each level developed by using data accumulated from more than 2,000,000 TOSEL test takers delegated at 15,000 schools and academies

CLASSIFIED AREAS OF INTELLIGENCE

Content designed to foster and expand the strengths of each student, categorized by the eight areas of intelligence

CONTINUITY

A complete course of English education ranging from kindergarten, elementary school, middle school, high schoool, and up to adults.

HIGH RELIABILITY

A high reliability level (Cronbach's alpha: .904 for elementary school students / .864 for university students) proven by several studies (Oxford University / Modern Language Journal)

SYSTEMATIC & EFFECTIVE ENGLISH EDUCATION

Accurate diagnosis and extensive materials which provide a step-by-step development in English learning, according to the quality of each learner's ability

TOSEL® Level Chart

Seven Separate Assessments

TOSEL divides the test into seven stages, by considering the test takers' cognitive levels, according to different ages. Unlike other assessments based on only one level, TOSEL includes separate assessments for preschool, elementary school, middle school, high school students, and for adults, which also includes both professionals and college students.

TOSEL's reporting system highlights the strengths and weaknesses of each test taker and suggests areas for further development.

COCOON

Suitable for children aged 4-6 (pre-schoolers)

The first step in the TOSEL system, the test is composed of colorful designs and interesting questions to interest young learners and to put them at ease.

Pre-STARTER

Suitable for children aged 7-8 (1st-2nd grades of elementary school)

Evaluates the ability to comprehend simple vocabulary, conversations, and sentences.

STARTER

Suitable for children aged 9-10 (3rd-4th grades of elementary school)

Evaluates the ability to comprehend short sentences and conversations related to everyday situations or topics.

BASIC

Suitable for children aged 11-12 (5th–6th grades of elementary school)

Evaluates the ability to communicate about personal information, daily activities, future plans, and past experiences in written and spoken language.

JUNIOR

Suitable for middle school students

Evaluates the ability to comprehend short paragraphs, practical texts, and speech covering general topics and to participate in simple daily conversations.

HIGH JUNIOR

Suitable for high school students

Evaluates the ability to use English fluently, accurately, and effectively on a wide range of social and academic subjects, as well as the ability to use sentences with a variety of complex structures.

ADVANCED

Suitable for university students and adults

Evaluates the ability to use practical English required for a job or work environment, as well as the ability to use and understand English at the university level.

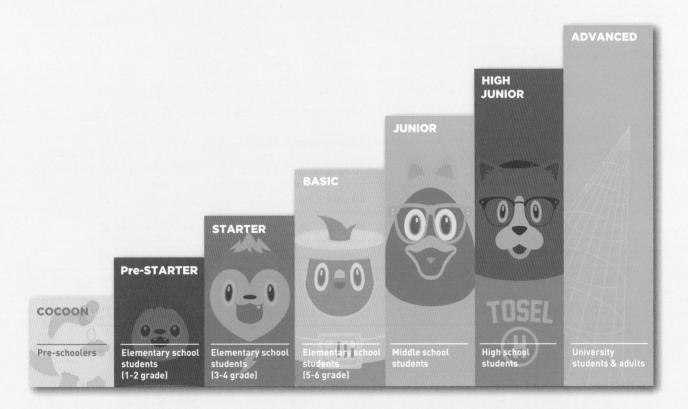

COCOON — Pre-schoolers

Pre-STARTER — Elementary school students (1-2 grade)

STARTER — Elementary school students (3-4 grade)

BASIC — Elementary school students (5-6 grade)

JUNIOR — Middle school students

HIGH JUNIOR — High school students

ADVANCED — University students & adults

Evaluation

Assessing the Four Skills

TOSEL evaluates the four language skills: reading, listening, speaking and writing, through indirect and direct assessment items.

This system of evaluation is part of a concerted effort to break away from materials geared solely toward grammar and reading-oriented education.

TOSEL Test Information

Level	Score	Grade	Section	
			Section I Listening & Speaking	Section II Reading & Writing
COCOON	100		15 Questions / 15 min	15 Questions / 15 min
Pre-STARTER	100		15 Questions / 15 min	20 Questions / 25 min
STARTER	100		20 Questions / 15 min	20 Questions / 25 min
BASIC	100	1-10	30 Questions / 20 min	30 Questions / 30 min
JUNIOR	100		30 Questions / 20 min	30 Questions / 30 min
HIGH JUNIOR	100		30 Questions / 25 min	35 Questions / 35 min
ADVANCED	990		70 Questions / 45 min	70 Questions / 55 min

Certificates

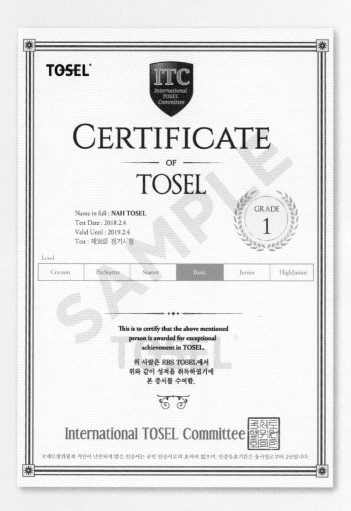

TOSEL Certificate

The International TOSEL Committee officially evaluates and certifies the level of English proficiency of English learners from the age of 4 to adults.

Certified by

Mar. 2010   Korea University

Dec. 2009   The Korean Society of Speech Science

Dec. 2009   The Korea Association of Foreign Language Education

Nov. 2009   The Applied Linguistics Association of Korea

Oct. 2009   The Pan Korea English Teachers Association

CHAPTER 1

Daily Life

UNIT 1

Teacher's Book p.100

Going to the Movies

What is your favorite movie?
When do you watch movies?

What do Ben and Riku like to do? They like to watch movies. What are they doing tonight? They want to go to a new movie theater. It is in the downtown area. The movie is an action movie. They love action movies. What time does the movie start? It starts at 7:45. So Ben and Riku have to be there by 7:30. But the theater is far. Ben and Riku need one hour to get there. They are taking the subway. First, Riku has to leave his house. He has to leave at 6:00. He has to arrive at Ben's house at 6:30. Then, they can go to the movie theater together.

New Words

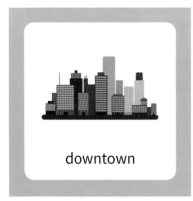

downtown

action movie

leave

arrive

Part A. Sentence Completion

1. _____ does the movie start?

   (A) Is

   (B) Can

   (C) Who

   (D) When

2. My home is far _____ the theater.

   (A) of

   (B) into

   (C) from

   (D) away

Part B. Situational Writing

3.  There is a theater _____.

   (A) in a forest

   (B) at the beach

   (C) in my village

   (D) in the downtown area

4.  He is _____ his house.

   (A) leaving

   (B) painting

   (C) building

   (D) cleaning

Field Trip Plan

8:30 AM   We leave the school.

9:00 AM   We arrive at the beach.

9:00 - 10:00 AM   We walk on the beach.

10:00 AM We leave the beach.

10:30 AM We arrive back at the school.

5. When do we arrive at the beach?

(A) 8:30 AM

(B) 9:00 AM

(C) 9:30 AM

(D) 10:00 AM

6. How long are we at the beach?

(A) 30 minutes

(B) 40 minutes

(C) 50 minutes

(D) 60 minutes

Part D. General Reading and Retelling

What do Ben and Riku like to do? They like to watch movies. What are they doing tonight? They want to go to a new movie theater. It is in the downtown area. The movie is an action movie. They love action movies. What time does the movie start? It starts at 7:45. So Ben and Riku have to be there by 7:30. But the theater is far. Ben and Riku need one hour to get there. They are taking the subway. First, Riku has to leave his house. He has to leave at 6:00. He has to arrive at Ben's house at 6:30. Then, they can go to the movie theater together.

7. What is the best title?

(A) Ben's Party
(B) Ben Plays Soccer
(C) Ben and Riku Shop
(D) Ben and Riku Go to the Movies

8. What kind of movies do Ben and Riku like?

(A) sad movies
(B) scary movies
(C) action movies
(D) music movies

9. What time does Riku leave his house?

(A) 6:00
(B) 6:30
(C) 7:00
(D) 7:45

10. What happens first?

(A) The movie starts.
(B) Riku arrives at Ben's house.
(C) Ben and Riku leave Ben's house.
(D) Ben and Riku arrive at the theater.

Listening Practice

 Listen and write.

  MP3 S2-1

Going to the Movies

What do Ben and Riku like to do? They like to watch movies. What are they doing tonight? They want to go to a new movie theater. It is in the

1 _____ area. The movie is an 2 _____ movie. They love action movies. What time does the movie start? It starts at 7:45. So Ben and Riku have to be there by 7:30. But the theater is far. Ben and Riku need one hour to get there. They are taking the subway. First, Riku

has to 3 _____ his house. He has to leave at 6:00. He has to

4 _____ at Ben's house at 6:30. Then, they can go to the movie theater together.

Word Bank

downtown	alive
leave	donton
liv	axion
action	arrive

 Listen. Pause. Say each sentence.

  MP3 S2-1G

✏️ Writing Practice

 Write the words.

1

2

3

4

📄 Write the words.

Summary

Ben and Riku are going to a new _____ in the downtown area.
They are going to watch an action movie. The theater is far. They are taking
the subway.

Word Puzzle

Y	Z	D	U	B	O	I	K	P	I	I	D	I	G	I
R	D	D	A	G	X	F	M	A	Y	T	R	W	G	P
Y	M	X	X	F	V	O	D	O	W	N	T	O	W	N
U	X	O	A	B	U	B	E	I	X	C	H	W	Z	T
Y	B	L	R	G	W	O	R	W	A	R	Z	G	U	J
X	U	O	R	D	C	D	D	B	C	Q	L	W	Y	B
X	L	P	I	J	V	F	J	A	T	Q	Y	W	Y	G
A	Q	S	V	U	G	Y	F	F	I	T	R	Q	I	I
Y	F	V	E	O	M	U	Q	L	O	X	D	M	T	C
V	E	A	E	B	F	I	O	W	N	M	G	H	J	L
S	Z	G	K	D	S	N	Y	S	M	Z	L	H	F	P
G	G	K	C	N	Q	P	E	K	O	S	E	Y	N	J
D	J	H	Z	A	D	N	D	F	V	H	A	P	W	C
Y	I	M	Q	K	K	S	D	W	I	L	V	V	T	E
T	S	Z	E	P	N	J	P	K	E	S	E	Q	Z	R

Write the words. Then find them in the puzzle.

1 _____   2 _____   3 _____   4 _____

UNIT 2

Teacher's Book
p.103

Tina's Day

What time do you go to school? Draw the time.
What time do you get home from school?
Draw the time.

What does Tina do every day? First, she wakes up. Then she makes her bed. After that, she goes into the bathroom. In the bathroom, she washes her face and hands. Her parents are waiting in the kitchen. Tina goes to the kitchen. She has breakfast. Then, she gets dressed and goes to school. At school, she studies many subjects. Then it is time for lunch. After lunch, she takes a short nap. Then she studies some more. Finally, she walks home. At home, her dad is in the kitchen. Tina says, "I am hungry!" Tina and her dad make a snack. Then it is time to read.

New Words

make the bed

wash your face

get dressed

make a snack

Part A. Sentence Completion

1. She _____ up early.

   (A) wake

   (B) wakes

   (C) is wake

   (D) waking

2. She cooks with _____ dad.

   (A) he

   (B) her

   (C) him

   (D) she

Part B. Situational Writing

3.    You should brush your teeth in the _____.

   (A) kitchen

   (B) bedroom

   (C) bathroom

   (D) dining room

4.    He is having a _____.

   (A) nap

   (B) rest

   (C) party

   (D) snack

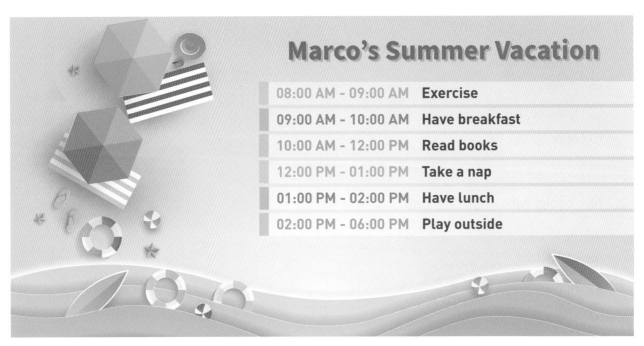

5. What does Marco do before breakfast?

(A) exercise

(B) take a nap

(C) read books

(D) meet friends

6. When does Marco have lunch?

(A) noon

(B) 12:30 PM

(C) 1:00 PM

(D) 2:30 PM

Part D. General Reading and Retelling

What does Tina do every day? First, she wakes up. Then she makes her bed. After that, she goes into the bathroom. In the bathroom, she washes her face and hands. Her parents are waiting in the kitchen. Tina goes to the kitchen. She has breakfast. Then, she gets dressed and goes to school. At school, she studies many subjects. Then it is time for lunch. After lunch, she takes a short nap. Then she studies some more. Finally, she walks home. At home, her dad is in the kitchen. Tina says, "I am hungry!" Tina and her dad make a snack. Then it is time to read.

7. What is the best title?

   (A) Tina's Day
   (B) Tina's Toys
   (C) Tina's School
   (D) Tina's Parents

8. What does Tina NOT do every day?

   (A) ride a bike
   (B) walk home
   (C) wash her face
   (D) make a snack

9. Where are Tina's parents in the morning?

   (A) in the kitchen
   (B) in the bathroom
   (C) in the living room
   (D) in the dining room

10. What does Tina do at school?

   (A) eat snacks
   (B) run in the gym
   (C) help the teacher
   (D) study many subjects

Listening Practice

 Listen and write.

  MP3 S2-2

Tina's Day

What does Tina do every day? First, she wakes up. Then she
¹ _____ her bed. After that, she goes into the bathroom. In the
bathroom, she ² _____ her face and hands. Her parents are
waiting in the kitchen. Tina goes to the kitchen. She has breakfast. Then,
she gets ³ _____ and goes to school. At school, she studies
many subjects. Then it is time for lunch. After lunch, she takes a short
nap. Then she studies some more. Finally, she walks home. At home, her
dad is in the kitchen. Tina says, "I am hungry!" Tina and her dad make a
⁴ _____ . Then it is time to read.

Word Bank

makes	washes
sneck	snack
meks	drest
wushes	dressed

 Listen. Pause. Say each sentence.

  MP3 S2-2G

Writing Practice

Write the words.

1 ⬚⬚⬚ ⬚⬚ ⬚⬚⬚

2 ⬚⬚⬚⬚ ⬚⬚⬚⬚ ⬚⬚⬚⬚

3 ⬚⬚⬚ ⬚⬚⬚⬚⬚⬚

4 ⬚⬚⬚⬚ ⬚⬚⬚ ⬚⬚⬚⬚⬚

 Write the words.

Summary

_____, Tina wakes up, gets ready for school, and has breakfast. At school, she studies and has lunch. She walks home. Her dad makes a snack.

Word Puzzle

X	W	Q	S	P	M	A	K	E	T	H	E	B	E	D
Z	K	J	S	F	C	X	Y	L	O	Q	D	F	E	E
S	V	W	F	M	S	U	P	S	J	W	R	P	K	G
I	L	O	Z	W	G	H	Y	P	W	E	O	J	A	L
A	D	Z	B	A	H	I	U	A	I	I	H	T	D	G
T	Y	T	P	S	Q	P	F	V	F	P	E	U	Z	E
F	B	A	L	H	Z	T	J	L	O	D	W	B	J	T
I	B	X	W	Y	H	R	G	F	E	V	J	W	B	D
S	B	Y	S	O	Z	T	S	V	E	Y	O	A	S	R
H	J	L	Z	U	I	T	U	U	T	M	R	L	I	E
T	M	Y	N	R	X	N	E	G	E	G	Z	U	B	S
Q	Q	H	Y	F	Y	O	A	S	M	I	C	K	M	S
M	A	K	E	A	S	N	A	C	K	G	X	I	K	E
X	Z	C	S	C	L	H	B	E	Z	I	B	V	F	D
K	H	G	G	E	U	Y	D	K	L	T	Y	L	V	U

 Write the words. Then find them in the puzzle.

1 _____ 2 _____ 3 _____ 4 _____

UNIT 3

Teacher's Book p.107

Jisoo Cleans Her Room

Think! Is your room messy?
Who cleans your room?

It is Sunday morning. Jisoo has no school. What does she want to do? She wants to read comic books. Jisoo sits down. She opens her comic book. But then she looks at her room. Oh no! Her room is very messy! Now Jisoo wants to clean the room. She stands up. She opens the window. The air is fresh. Then she looks at the floor. Her clothes are on the floor. She hangs her clothes in her closet. What does Jisoo do next? She cleans her desk. She puts her books on her bookshelf. Finally, she mops the floor. Now, Jisoo's room is clean. She feels great. It is a perfect Sunday morning. Now she can read her comic book.

New Words

fresh

closet

bookshelf

mop

Part A. Sentence Completion

 10 minutes

1. What _____ on the floor?

   (A) is

   (B) be

   (C) can

   (D) make

2. Put your clothes _____ your closet.

   (A) in

   (B) for

   (C) out

   (D) in front

Part B. Situational Writing

3.  There are so many books on the _____.

   (A)   floor

   (B)   desk

   (C)   closet

   (D)   bookshelf

4.  He _____ the floor.

   (A)   mops

   (B)   colors

   (C)   paints

   (D)   draws

Misha's Day

- feed the cat
- walk the dog
- take the trash out
- do the laundry
- wash the dishes

5. What is Misha doing today?

   (A) washing the car

   (B) feeding the fish

   (C) doing the laundry

   (D) mopping the floor

6. What is Misha NOT doing today?

   (A) walking the dog

   (B) washing the dishes

   (C) taking the trash out

   (D) cleaning the kitchen

Part D. General Reading and Retelling

It is Sunday morning. Jisoo has no school. What does she want to do? She wants to read comic books. Jisoo sits down. She opens her comic book. But then she looks at her room. Oh no! Her room is very messy! Now Jisoo wants to clean the room. She stands up. She opens the window. The air is fresh. Then she looks at the floor. Her clothes are on the floor. She hangs her clothes in her closet. What does Jisoo do next? She cleans her desk. She puts her books on her bookshelf. Finally, she mops the floor. Now, Jisoo's room is clean. She feels great. It is a perfect Sunday morning. Now she can read her comic book.

7. What is the best title?

   (A) Jisoo's New Dog
   (B) Jisoo's Fun Saturday
   (C) Jisoo Goes to the Park
   (D) Jisoo Cleans Her Room

8. What does Jisoo NOT do today?

   (A) go to school
   (B) clean her desk
   (C) open a window
   (D) open a comic book

9. How does Jisoo's room change?

   (A) big → small
   (B) small → big
   (C) clean → dirty
   (D) messy → clean

10. Where does Jisoo put her clothes?

   (A) on the floor
   (B) in her closet
   (C) on her bookshelf
   (D) out of the window

Listening Practice

 Listen and write.

  MP3 S2-3

Jisoo Cleans Her Room

It is Sunday morning. Jisoo has no school. What does she want to do? She
wants to read comic books. Jisoo sits down. She opens her comic book.
But then she looks at her room. Oh no! Her room is very messy! Now Jisoo
wants to clean the room. She stands up. She opens the window. The air is
¹ _____ . Then she looks at the floor. Her clothes are on the floor.
She hangs her clothes in her ² _____ . What does Jisoo do next?
She cleans her desk. She puts her books on her ³ _____ . Finally,
she ⁴ _____ the floor. Now, Jisoo's room is clean. She feels great.
It is a perfect Sunday morning. Now she can read her comic book.

Word Bank

clozet	bookshelf
fresh	closet
mopps	flesh
bookself	mops

 Listen. Pause. Say each sentence.

  MP3 S2-3G

Writing Practice

 Write the words.

1

2

3

4

 Write the words.

Summary

Jisoo wants to read a comic book. But her room is messy. She opens the
window and hangs her clothes in her _____. She cleans her
desk, puts her books on the bookshelf, and mops the floor.

Word Puzzle

G	K	R	J	X	G	C	I	H	W	D	M	O	T	P
S	M	O	P	H	H	L	M	Z	C	L	O	S	E	T
Y	G	L	P	O	X	Z	P	P	Q	P	O	I	Z	N
M	K	P	W	A	B	O	O	K	S	H	E	L	F	W
Q	S	N	N	R	I	O	A	W	Z	V	M	I	Y	Q
I	J	B	R	J	Y	F	Q	L	W	I	C	A	F	O
I	R	U	B	G	A	F	G	T	N	W	N	J	O	L
F	U	K	C	S	R	T	T	A	W	J	T	B	A
W	T	Y	U	I	R	E	P	G	G	H	D	H	Y	E
O	P	H	A	R	C	S	N	U	Q	C	N	J	P	D
F	O	Q	K	T	P	H	W	T	S	Y	N	G	X	G
H	M	Q	B	O	I	K	C	U	V	A	E	V	Q	P
T	N	S	E	K	O	T	A	J	A	Z	V	Y	L	N
V	U	Y	J	U	O	W	K	S	M	D	P	W	I	W
K	K	R	H	U	L	L	Y	S	L	P	L	Q	F	G

🔍 Write the words. Then find them in the puzzle.

1 _____

2 _____

3 _____

4 _____

UNIT 4

At Blue Mountain

Do you like to go to the mountains?
Which mountain do you like best?

Every February is special for Nolan's family. They go to Blue Mountain. They stay there one night. They pack food and drinks. It is cold at the mountain. They wear warm jackets. Nolan's family arrives at a small house. They unpack their bags. Nolan's father cooks dinner. And Nolan helps his father. They cook mushroom soup. Nolan's mother goes out and gets wood. She makes a fire. The fire is in the chimney. It gets warm inside the house. Nolan's sister walks around the forest. She takes some photos. After dinner, Nolan's family plays a board game. They have a great time at Blue Mountain.

New Words

pack

arrive at

chimney

have a great time

Part A. **Sentence Completion**

1. They stay there one _____.

    (A) night

    (B) nights

    (C) a night

    (D) my night

2. It is cold _____ winter.

    (A) in

    (B) at

    (C) under

    (D) above

Part B. **Situational Writing**

3.

We need some _____.

    (A) salt

    (B) sand

    (C) wood

    (D) water

4.

They are playing _____ together.

    (A) soccer

    (B) basketball

    (C) a board game

    (D) a computer game

What Do They Do on the Weekend?

Austin
I like music a lot. Every weekend, I go to Satton Hall. Rachel Gugu always plays concerts there. She is my favorite singer.

Kelly
I never stay at home. My sister likes badminton. So we play badminton in the park.

Myra
I visit my grandparents. They have a strawberry farm. I pick strawberries there. And I make a strawberry jam.

5. Who stays home all weekend?

   (A) Austin

   (B) Kelly

   (C) Myra

   (D) no one

6. What is true?

   (A) Myra picks apples.

   (B) Kelly plays badminton.

   (C) Austin plays in a band.

   (D) Myra makes strawberry pies.

Part D. **General Reading and Retelling**

Every February is special for Nolan's family. They go to Blue Mountain. They stay there one night. They pack food and drinks. It is cold at the mountain. They wear warm jackets. Nolan's family arrives at a small house. They unpack their bags. Nolan's father cooks dinner. And Nolan helps his father. They cook mushroom soup. Nolan's mother goes out and gets wood. She makes a fire. The fire is in the chimney. It gets warm inside the house. Nolan's sister walks around the forest. She takes some photos. After dinner, Nolan's family plays a board game. They have a great time at Blue Mountain.

7. What is the best title?

(A) A Family Trip

(B) A Cooking Class

(C) A Fun Day at School

(D) Summer at the Beach

8. Who makes soup?

(A) Nolan's uncle

(B) Nolan's sister

(C) Nolan's mother

(D) Nolan and his father

9. What does Nolan's mother do?

(A) get wood

(B) take photos

(C) make a house

(D) find mushrooms

10. What does Blue Mountain have?

(A) a big pool

(B) cold weather

(C) large houses

(D) a flower garden

Listening Practice

 Listen and write.

  MP3 S2-4

At Blue Mountain

Every February is special for Nolan's family. They go to Blue Mountain.
They stay there one night. They [¹ _____] food and drinks.
It is cold at the mountain. They wear warm jackets. Nolan's family
[² _____] at a small house. They unpack their bags. Nolan's father
cooks dinner. And Nolan helps his father. They cook mushroom soup.
Nolan's mother goes out and gets wood. She makes a fire. The fire is in
the [³ _____]. It gets warm inside the house. Nolan's sister walks
around the forest. She takes some photos. After dinner, Nolan's family
plays a board game. They have a [⁴ _____] time at Blue Mountain.

Word Bank

great	alives
pack	chimey
pak	arrives
gret	chimney

 Listen. Pause. Say each sentence.

  MP3 S2-4G

✏️ Writing Practice

 Write the words.

1 ⬜⬜⬜

2 ⬜⬜⬜⬜⬜ ⬜⬜

3 ⬜⬜⬜⬜⬜

4 ⬜⬜⬜ ⬜⬜⬜⬜ ⬜⬜⬜

 Write the words.

Summary

Every February, Nolan's family goes on a _____ to Blue Mountain. They cook dinner, make a fire, take some photos, and play a board game. They have a great time.

Word Puzzle

A	N	H	K	Y	N	W	V	U	P	Y	W	M	U	Y
G	A	A	D	G	P	U	S	S	U	H	L	W	F	Q
I	I	V	E	U	N	C	E	J	B	E	B	W	D	A
C	F	E	A	H	R	D	R	X	L	C	X	A	D	S
D	E	A	X	Z	H	N	Q	T	V	H	Q	R	R	X
T	D	G	D	C	N	Q	F	O	T	I	S	R	I	M
V	U	R	Q	Y	T	S	J	Y	Y	M	N	I	D	Q
W	J	E	Z	E	J	E	O	A	D	N	O	V	E	E
U	I	A	S	O	P	Z	C	V	P	E	Z	E	T	F
T	M	T	K	X	R	H	X	X	I	Y	A	A	K	U
E	P	T	Z	P	A	C	K	Q	A	U	T	T	D	M
L	D	I	I	M	Y	N	I	U	C	X	T	B	R	C
M	S	M	C	U	Q	I	B	G	K	S	K	E	V	Y
U	X	E	X	X	C	M	Q	R	G	E	V	A	L	M
A	G	O	A	M	L	A	A	J	M	U	H	X	W	M

Write the words. Then find them in the puzzle.

1 _____

2 _____

3 _____

4 _____

Match the pictures to the correct words.

Teacher's Book p.115

action movie

arrive

arrive at

bookshelf

chimney

closet

downtown

fresh

get dressed

have a great time

leave

make a snack

make the bed

mop

pack

wash your face

CHAPTER 2

House

UNIT 5

Lea's Dream House

Teacher's Book
p.116

Do you have a dream house? What is it like?

Lea lives in a big city. She lives by the airport. But Lea hates the noise. What is Lea's dream home? It is in the country. It has a big yard. Lea's dog can run in the yard. What is inside the house? There is a big living room. In the living room, there is a big TV. There is a sofa and two big chairs. They are green. In the kitchen, there is a big table. There are four chairs. There are also big windows. It is very bright in the kitchen. What is in the bedroom? Lea wants a large, soft bed. And she wants a blue carpet on the floor. Lea wants a warm home. This is Lea's dream home.

New Words

country

yard

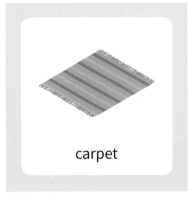

carpet

window

Part A. Sentence Completion

1. _____ are you going now? Are you going to school?

   (A) Who

   (B) What

   (C) Which

   (D) Where

2. What _____ she want? She wants a dog.

   (A) do

   (B) is

   (C) to be

   (D) does

Part B. Situational Writing

3.  There is a _____ on the floor.

   (A) cake

   (B) cookie

   (C) carpet

   (D) curtain

4.  A dog is running in the _____.

   (A) yard

   (B) forest

   (C) kitchen

   (D) living room

Zack's Dream Room　　　Gary's Dream Room

5. Which dream room has toy blocks?

   (A) Zack's

   (B) Gary's

   (C) both

   (D) no one

6. Which is NOT in Gary's dream room?

   (A) a window

   (B) a blue wall

   (C) a computer

   (D) a yellow carpet

Part D. General Reading and Retelling

Lea lives in a big city. She lives by the airport. But Lea hates the noise. What is Lea's dream home? It is in the country. It has a big yard. Lea's dog can run in the yard. What is inside the house? There is a big living room. In the living room, there is a big TV. There is a sofa and two big chairs. They are green. In the kitchen, there is a big table. There are four chairs. There are also big windows. It is very bright in the kitchen. What is in the bedroom? Lea wants a large, soft bed. And she wants a blue carpet on the floor. Lea wants a warm home. This is Lea's dream home.

7. What is the best title?

(A) Lea's Dream Job

(B) Lea's Dream House

(C) Lea's Favorite Puppy

(D) Lea's Last Night Dream

8. Where does Lea want to live?

(A) in a big city

(B) by a beach

(C) by an airport

(D) in the country

9. Which pet does Lea want?

(A) a cat

(B) a fish

(C) a dog

(D) a bird

10. What is in Lea's dream home?

(A) two beds

(B) purple chairs

(C) a blue carpet

(D) a small living room

Listening Practice

 Listen and write.

  MP3 S2-5

Lea's Dream House

Lea lives in a big city. She lives by the airport. But Lea hates the noise.

What is Lea's dream home? It is in the ¹ _____ . It has a big yard.

Lea's dog can run in the ² _____ . What is inside the house?

There is a big living room. In the living room, there is a big TV. There is a

sofa and two big chairs. They are green. In the kitchen, there is a big table.

There are four chairs. There are also big ³ _____ . It is very bright

in the kitchen. What is in the bedroom? Lea wants a large, soft bed. And

she wants a blue ⁴ _____ on the floor. Lea wants a warm home.

This is Lea's dream home.

Word Bank

yard	windo
windows	contry
country	carpat
yad	carpet

 Listen. Pause. Say each sentence.

  MP3 S2-5G

Writing Practice

 Write the words.

1

2

3

4

Write the words.

Summary

Lea lives in a big city, but she hates the noise. She wants a house in the country with a big yard. That is Lea's _____ house.

Word Puzzle

J	X	S	B	B	T	D	D	Q	K	S	W	A	Y	Y
I	P	L	Z	W	A	J	K	W	M	Y	I	S	D	G
A	E	V	B	P	C	E	R	H	R	X	K	E	U	F
Y	N	O	Y	E	O	D	O	C	X	X	S	B	D	Y
Y	D	Q	O	A	U	M	S	D	W	K	Q	T	L	J
Z	Q	A	C	K	N	T	W	U	M	L	C	R	C	X
F	J	N	A	F	T	B	C	C	O	U	X	S	T	E
X	S	M	R	Y	R	B	O	W	C	Y	T	M	H	H
Y	Q	U	P	G	Y	T	B	I	I	T	T	W	Z	N
D	X	W	E	H	C	J	T	N	T	C	C	Y	F	T
M	J	J	T	O	F	U	A	D	U	R	I	P	L	T
W	C	P	Q	A	R	T	J	O	S	V	U	E	M	Q
T	Y	A	R	D	G	P	E	W	R	B	J	X	F	R
A	R	I	C	P	X	W	U	S	Z	K	S	G	X	M
W	D	K	J	N	I	D	Q	M	E	Y	R	O	T	H

🔍 Write the words. Then find them in the puzzle.

  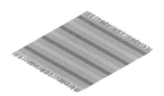 

1 _____

2 _____

3 _____

4 _____

UNIT 6

Milo Sits in Chairs

Name three things in your house.
Where are they in the house?

Milo is Katia's dog. He loves to sit in chairs. There are three big chairs in the house. Every day, Milo sits in all the chairs. In the morning, he sits in the purple chair. It is in the living room. From the purple chair, Milo can see a bookshelf. It is across from the purple chair. There are five books. Milo cannot read. But he looks at the books. In the afternoon, Milo sits in the dark blue chair. It is in the kitchen. Milo can look at the stove. Pots and pans are on the stove. In the evening, Milo sits in the light pink chair. That chair is in the bedroom. It is by the bed. Katia also sits there.

New Words

chair

bookshelf

across from

stove

Part A. Sentence Completion

1. Look at this table. _____ is purple.

   (A) It

   (B) It's

   (C) Their

   (D) These

2. _____ can you see? I can see some books.

   (A) Who

   (B) That

   (C) What

   (D) Where

Part B. Situational Writing

3.  The blue house is _____ the school.

   (A) under

   (B) above

   (C) next to

   (D) across from

4.  The bookshelf is _____ the sofa.

   (A) on

   (B) under

   (C) next to

   (D) across from

Brooklyn Furniture Shop is on Sale!

Sofa	Lamp	Drawers	Bookshelf	Mirror	Bathtub
$80 → **$70**	$25 → **$22**	$50 → **$47**	$40 → **$35**	$10 → **$8**	$73 → **$68**

5. What is the most expensive?

(A) the sofa

(B) the lamp

(C) the mirror

(D) the bathtub

6. What is NOT on sale?

(A) a lamp

(B) a mirror

(C) a stove

(D) a bookshelf

Part D. General Reading and Retelling

Milo is Katia's dog. He loves to sit in chairs. There are three big chairs in the house. Every day, Milo sits in all the chairs. In the morning, he sits in the purple chair. It is in the living room. From the purple chair, Milo can see a bookshelf. It is across from the purple chair. There are five books. Milo cannot read. But he looks at the books. In the afternoon, Milo sits in the dark blue chair. It is in the kitchen. Milo can look at the stove. Pots and pans are on the stove. In the evening, Milo sits in the light pink chair. That chair is in the bedroom. It is by the bed. Katia also sits there.

7. What is the best title?

  (A) Milo Goes to School

  (B) Milo and Three Chairs

  (C) Katia Gets a New Dog

  (D) Katia and Milo Buy a Chair

8. What does Milo like to do?

  (A) sit in chairs

  (B) take pictures

  (C) make furniture

  (D) go outside for walks

9. What chair is NOT in the house?

  (A) a purple one

  (B) a dark blue one

  (C) a light blue one

  (D) a light pink one

10. What does Milo do in the living room?

  (A) read to Katia

  (B) look at books

  (C) sit in a pink chair

  (D) see pots and pans

Listening Practice

 Listen and write.

 MP3 S2-6

Milo Sits in Chairs

Milo is Katia's dog. He loves to sit in ¹_____. There are three big
chairs in the house. Every day, Milo sits in all the chairs. In the morning,
he sits in the purple chair. It is in the living room. From the purple chair,
Milo can see a ²_____. It is ³_____ from the purple
chair. There are five books. Milo cannot read. But he looks at the books.
In the afternoon, Milo sits in the dark blue chair. It is in the kitchen. Milo
can look at the ⁴_____. Pots and pans are on the stove. In the
evening, Milo sits in the light pink chair. That chair is in the bedroom. It is
by the bed. Katia also sits there.

Word Bank

stove	chers
stov	chairs
across	acros
bokshelf	bookshelf

 Listen. Pause. Say each sentence.

 MP3 S2-6G

Writing Practice

 Write the words.

1

2

3

4

 Write the words.

Summary

Milo is a dog. He sits in three big _____ every day. There are

chairs in the living room, kitchen, and bedroom.

Word Puzzle

Y	E	T	T	F	H	E	W	I	X	H	J	O	D	T
U	F	U	M	C	K	Q	Y	O	Q	H	C	Y	Y	M
U	B	N	M	C	C	Y	G	V	M	Q	C	U	A	R
M	R	F	G	M	M	C	G	O	Q	G	E	J	C	Q
T	B	B	P	M	I	H	J	E	C	U	G	M	R	X
K	A	O	K	C	P	X	W	W	Q	Z	C	D	O	Y
Y	B	O	Q	W	Y	M	M	C	Z	G	H	Z	S	S
O	G	K	V	V	C	N	K	I	A	B	A	F	S	S
C	Q	S	J	C	H	A	I	R	U	K	E	O	F	Z
P	G	H	L	O	L	M	K	J	C	V	S	P	R	Q
O	E	E	E	A	K	H	I	O	A	J	T	W	O	B
G	B	L	S	H	S	O	P	U	Q	H	O	B	M	H
D	X	F	B	D	E	L	K	C	V	U	V	J	X	P
M	V	Q	Z	X	G	E	W	U	L	R	E	W	H	R
B	P	N	O	R	G	A	E	J	Q	F	P	J	U	Q

 Write the words. Then find them in the puzzle.

1 _____ 2 _____ 3 _____ 4 _____

UNIT 7

Teacher's Book p.124

Show and Tell Class

Think! You have a box.
A special thing is in the box. What is it?

Today, the class has "Show and Tell." What is "Show and Tell"? Students bring a special thing from home. They can bring anything. They show the special things to their friends. Then they talk about it. Carl is first. He shows his earphones to the class. He says, "I like listening to music. So these earphones are special to me." Then, it is Bobby's turn. Bobby shows a picture. He says, "This is my family. I love all of them. They are very special to me." Clara goes next. She shows a small notebook. She says, "This is my diary. I write in it every night. It is the most special thing to me." All the students bring their special things!

New Words

earphones

special

picture

diary

Part A. Sentence Completion

1. _____ are my friends.

   (A) He

   (B) This

   (C) That

   (D) These

2. Where is _____ diary?

   (A) I

   (B) my

   (C) me

   (D) mine

Part B. Situational Writing

3.  There are many _____ on the wall.

   (A)   vases

   (B)   flowers

   (C)   pictures

   (D)   cameras

4.  I need a new _____.

   (A)   pencil

   (B)   textbook

   (C)   notebook

   (D)   bookmark

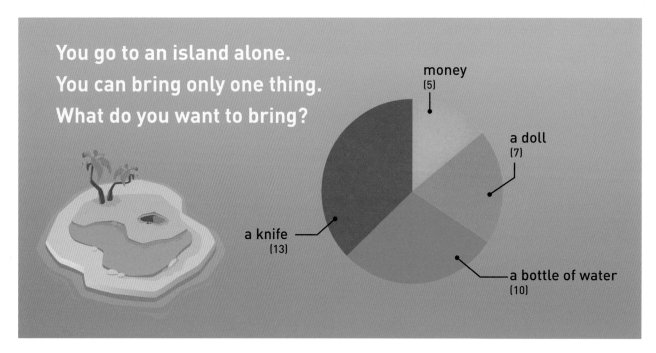

5. How many students want to bring money?

   (A) 5

   (B) 7

   (C) 10

   (D) 13

6. What are students NOT bringing?

   (A) water

   (B) a doll

   (C) snack

   (D) a knife

Part D. General Reading and Retelling

Today, the class has "Show and Tell." What is "Show and Tell"? Students bring a special thing from home. They can bring anything. They show the special things to their friends. Then they talk about it. Carl is first. He shows his earphones to the class. He says, "I like listening to music. So these earphones are special to me." Then, it is Bobby's turn. Bobby shows a picture. He says, "This is my family. I love all of them. They are very special to me." Clara goes next. She shows a small notebook. She says, "This is my diary. I write in it every night. It is the most special thing to me." All the students bring their special things!

7. What is the best title?

   (A) A Magic Show
   (B) Show and Tell
   (C) Carl Plays Music
   (D) A Book of Paintings

8. Why are the earphones special to Carl?

   (A) They are new.
   (B) They are expensive.
   (C) He likes listening to music.
   (D) His grandma also uses them.

9. What does Bobby bring?

   (A) a diary
   (B) a picture
   (C) an album
   (D) an orange

10. When does Clara write in her diary?

   (A) at night
   (B) at noon
   (C) during class
   (D) in the morning

Listening Practice

 Listen and write.

  MP3 S2-7

Show and Tell Class

Today, the class has "Show and Tell." What is "Show and Tell"? Students bring a ¹ _____ thing from home. They can bring anything. They show the special things to their friends. Then they talk about it. Carl is first. He shows his ² _____ to the class. He says, "I like listening to music. So these earphones are special to me." Then, it is Bobby's turn. Bobby shows a ³ _____. He says, "This is my family. I love all of them. They are very special to me." Clara goes next. She shows a small notebook. She says, "This is my ⁴ _____. I write in it every night. It is the most special thing to me." All the students bring their special things!

Word Bank

picture	special
earphones	piksure
diary	diery
speshul	earfones

 Listen. Pause. Say each sentence.

  MP3 S2-7G

Writing Practice

 Write the words.

1

2

3

4

 Write the words.

Summary

Today is "Show and Tell" in class. The students bring _____

things from home. They show the things to their friends. They talk about

them.

V	U	G	E	G	M	Y	X	P	F	Y	N	V	K	R
Z	U	G	D	U	V	I	V	Z	W	A	B	D	U	U
V	Z	C	V	Z	W	E	K	W	P	J	U	M	Q	C
V	S	P	E	C	I	A	L	O	M	B	Z	V	S	J
W	L	D	G	B	O	R	Y	J	E	M	L	J	P	M
E	M	Y	S	I	I	P	J	O	R	M	E	F	L	P
H	L	Y	L	V	X	H	C	C	P	O	S	G	Z	I
U	J	X	X	G	Z	O	A	N	L	O	T	T	P	C
M	G	Q	V	M	U	N	G	E	R	M	Y	Z	R	T
E	O	W	F	K	W	E	U	G	R	B	C	Y	I	U
X	K	D	B	Z	H	S	A	I	N	I	V	G	S	R
T	K	I	M	D	Z	N	B	Z	R	M	D	O	E	E
Y	G	A	H	M	H	Y	B	H	K	M	S	Q	I	L
V	W	R	G	Z	R	T	S	I	A	D	L	M	N	L
I	D	Y	X	P	J	B	D	L	A	U	C	D	M	D

 Write the words. Then find them in the puzzle.

   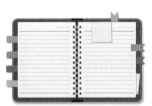

1 _____   2 _____   3 _____   4 _____

UNIT 8

 Teacher's Book p.128

Summer Vacation

Think! It is your vacation.
Where do you want to go?
What do you want to do?

Summer vacation is coming! Where is Rosa's family going? Today they choose. They are in the living room. Rosa's mother says, "Where do you want to go?" Rosa says, "My favorite place is the beach. I want to swim there!" Rosa's brother says, "The beach is too hot. My favorite place is the forest. There are many trees there. The air is fresh and cool. Let's go to the forest." Rosa's father says, "How about a water park? You can both swim there. Also, it is not too hot. There are many swimming pools. One pool is inside a building." Rosa's mother likes his idea. And Rosa and her brother also like it. Summer vacation is at the water park!

New Words

beach

forest

water park

inside

Part A. Sentence Completion

1. _____ many trees in the garden.

   (A) It are

   (B) They is

   (C) There is

   (D) There are

2. I _____ swim very fast.

   (A) is

   (B) be

   (C) am

   (D) can

Part B. Situational Writing

3.

   I want to lie on the _____.

   (A) bed

   (B) sofa

   (C) grass

   (D) beach

4.

   The boy hides _____ the box.

   (A) under

   (B) inside

   (C) next to

   (D) outside

5. What is the orange cat's favorite place?

    (A) on a hat

    (B) on a pot

    (C) inside a bag

    (D) inside a basket

6. Who likes to be in a basket?

    (A) the white cat

    (B) the black cat

    (C) the brown cat

    (D) the orange cat

Part D. General Reading and Retelling

Summer vacation is coming! Where is Rosa's family going? Today they choose. They are in the living room. Rosa's mother says, "Where do you want to go?" Rosa says, "My favorite place is the beach. I want to swim there!" Rosa's brother says, "The beach is too hot. My favorite place is the forest. There are many trees there. The air is fresh and cool. Let's go to the forest." Rosa's father says, "How about a water park? You can both swim there. Also, it is not too hot. There are many swimming pools. One pool is inside a building." Rosa's mother likes his idea. And Rosa and her brother also like it. Summer vacation is at the water park!

7. What is the best title?

   (A) Rosa's Favorite Place

   (B) How to Swim in a Pool

   (C) Many Trees and Fresh Air

   (D) Rosa's Family Plans a Vacation

8. Where do Rosa's family talk?

   (A) at a beach

   (B) in the forest

   (C) at a water park

   (D) in their living room

9. Why does Rosa like the beach?

   (A) She likes blue.

   (B) She likes to swim.

   (C) She likes fresh air.

   (D) She likes hot weather.

10. What is most likely true about Rosa's brother?

   (A) He cannot swim.

   (B) He likes the park.

   (C) He hates hot weather.

   (D) He wants to go to the beach.

Listening Practice

 Listen and write.

  MP3 S2-8

Summer Vacation

Summer vacation is coming! Where is Rosa's family going? Today they choose. They are in the living room. Rosa's mother says, "Where do you want to go?" Rosa says, "My favorite place is the ¹ _____ . I want to swim there!" Rosa's brother says, "The beach is too hot. My favorite place is the ² _____ . There are many trees there. The air is fresh and cool. Let's go to the forest." Rosa's father says, "How about a ³ _____ park? You can both swim there. Also, it is not too hot. There are many swimming pools. One pool is ⁴ _____ a building." Rosa's mother likes his idea. And Rosa and her brother also like it. Summer vacation is at the water park!

Word Bank

watter	forest
inside	porest
bich	beach
water	enside

 Listen. Pause. Say each sentence.

  MP3 S2-8G

Writing Practice

 Write the words.

1

2

3

4

 Write the words.

Summary

Rosa's family makes a _____ plan. They talk in the living room. They are going to a water park.

Word Puzzle

X	P	Y	R	R	W	A	T	E	R	P	A	R	K	U
A	Q	D	G	M	S	O	F	C	H	N	J	N	V	E
E	T	U	X	A	B	L	C	B	K	K	E	X	V	V
R	G	C	O	M	A	P	Z	Z	H	I	L	Y	N	T
Q	I	Z	F	N	C	I	N	B	H	Z	Z	K	D	B
G	W	I	O	G	V	N	I	Y	Q	J	F	O	Y	L
I	Z	C	Q	W	W	S	Z	T	M	E	H	N	C	Z
G	N	P	X	E	E	I	T	F	O	R	E	S	T	D
B	Z	M	J	S	Q	D	G	L	O	S	R	B	M	E
J	L	Y	N	K	M	E	L	O	B	E	X	N	L	U
J	V	C	B	A	J	F	Y	J	H	O	H	F	F	E
L	Z	F	E	J	O	N	V	L	Q	Z	O	T	S	O
L	D	E	A	M	L	C	F	V	R	S	U	W	A
V	K	Q	C	R	W	P	C	L	I	K	S	Z	W	I
S	V	H	H	E	J	B	X	T	D	A	L	G	V	O

 Write the words. Then find them in the puzzle.

1 _____   2 _____   3 _____   4 _____

Match the pictures to the correct words.

 Teacher's Book p.132

across from

beach

bookshelf

(carpet)

chair

country

diary

earphones

forest

inside

picture

special

stove

water park

window

yard

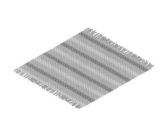

CHAPTER 3
Family Occasion

Teacher's Book
p.133

UNIT 9

Grandma's Birthday

Name a person in your family.
It is that person's birthday. Is there a cake?
How many candles are on it?

It is Grandma's birthday! What do we do for Grandma? First, we make a cake. Her favorite is carrot cake. I do not like carrot cake. My brother, Riku, does not like carrot cake. My parents do not like carrot cake. But Grandma likes it. So we make carrot cake. What is on the cake? There are many candles. This year, there are seventy candles. We bring Grandma the cake. We sing to her. Then she blows on the candles. But there are too many candles. Riku helps. Finally, the flames are out. Then we eat the cake. Grandma asks, "How is the cake?" We smile. We say, "This cake is delicious!" Because we know Grandma likes carrot cake. Then Grandma is happy.

New Words

carrot

candle

flame

delicious

Part A. Sentence Completion

1. It is Grandma's birthday. We make _____ favorite cake.

   (A) her

   (B) you

   (C) him

   (D) mine

2. _____ many candles are on the cake?

   (A) How

   (B) Who

   (C) What

   (D) Where

Part B. Situational Writing

3.  _____ on the candles. Make a wish!

   (A) Sit

   (B) Blow

   (C) Write

   (D) Stand

4.  The candle _____ is very bright!

   (A) sun

   (B) camp

   (C) flame

   (D) phone

	SUN	MON	TUE	WED	THU	FRI	SAT
					Jenny's birthday 1	2	3
	4	5	6	7	8	9	Dane's birthday 10
	11	Hazel's birthday 12	13	14	15	16	17
	18	19	20	Ayden's birthday 21	22	23	24
	25	26	27	28			

Whose birthday is in February?

5. When is Jenny's birthday?

(A) Thursday, February 1st

(B) Friday, February 2nd

(C) Saturday, February 1st

(D) Tuesday, February 2nd

6. Whose birthday is on the weekend?

(A) Jenny

(B) Dane

(C) Hazel

(D) Ayden

Part D. General Reading and Retelling

It is Grandma's birthday! What do we do for Grandma? First, we make a cake. Her favorite is carrot cake. I do not like carrot cake. My brother, Riku, does not like carrot cake. My parents do not like carrot cake. But Grandma likes it. So we make carrot cake. What is on the cake? There are many candles. This year, there are seventy candles. We bring Grandma the cake. We sing to her. Then she blows on the candles. But there are too many candles. Riku helps. Finally, the flames are out. Then we eat the cake. Grandma asks, "How is the cake?" We smile. We say, "This cake is delicious!" Because we know Grandma likes carrot cake. Then Grandma is happy.

7. What is the best title?

(A) Making a Cake
(B) Grandma's Birthday
(C) Carrots in the Garden
(D) Finding Grandma's Gift

8. What kind of cake does Grandma like?

(A) carrot
(B) coffee
(C) cheese
(D) chocolate

9. How old is Grandma?

(A) 50
(B) 60
(C) 70
(D) 80

10. Who is Riku?

(A) the writer
(B) Grandma's dog
(C) the writer's brother
(D) Grandma's brother

 Listen and write.

  MP3 S2-9

Grandma's Birthday

It is Grandma's birthday! What do we do for Grandma? First, we make a cake. Her favorite is ¹_____ cake. I do not like carrot cake. My brother, Riku, does not like carrot cake. My parents do not like carrot cake. But Grandma likes it. So we make carrot cake. What is on the cake?

There are many ²_____ . This year, there are seventy candles. We bring Grandma the cake. We sing to her. Then she blows on the candles.

But there are too many candles. Riku helps. Finally, the ³_____ are out. Then we eat the cake. Grandma asks, "How is the cake?" We smile. We say, "This cake is ⁴_____ !" Because we know Grandma likes carrot cake. Then Grandma is happy.

Word Bank

carots	delicious
carrot	delisious
frames	candels
flames	candles

 Listen. Pause. Say each sentence.

  MP3 S2-9G

Writing Practice

 Write the words.

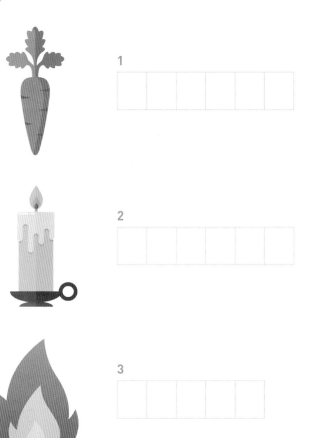

1
2
3
4

 Write the words.

Summary

Today is Grandma's birthday. We make a carrot cake for her. We put seventy

_____ on the cake. We sing. Grandma blows out the candles.

Word Puzzle

X	M	Z	N	P	C	C	J	A	J	P	D	R	Y	A
T	Q	L	G	W	X	H	T	T	M	G	E	A	T	J
Y	L	V	G	Z	I	M	Z	I	W	L	L	L	O	X
B	U	T	D	D	O	I	I	X	I	W	I	A	D	K
W	F	L	A	M	E	X	I	W	C	K	C	F	U	B
W	X	B	T	D	J	H	Q	V	A	E	I	I	A	L
X	H	L	X	D	T	D	E	Z	N	O	O	Y	I	H
V	N	K	L	Q	T	B	B	V	D	C	U	E	P	K
O	F	D	S	N	L	C	R	G	L	V	S	T	J	B
N	D	V	K	X	C	L	D	G	E	A	K	P	M	Y
F	L	C	A	R	R	O	T	X	J	Z	B	C	A	J
W	C	U	B	L	F	J	W	E	U	B	P	U	K	G
G	C	H	W	V	S	G	H	Z	L	R	L	W	V	R
V	K	K	D	I	H	H	T	L	C	E	T	A	H	Z
G	E	A	D	C	O	H	C	E	V	K	O	Q	T	J

 Write the words. Then find them in the puzzle.

1 _____

2 _____

3 _____

4 _____

UNIT 10

Teacher's Book
p.137

Eating Out vs. Eating at Home

Which do you like: eating at home or eating out?

Ruby is hungry. She knows a new restaurant. The restaurant is called "Fat Noodles." Ruby wants to eat at Fat Noodles. She finds her mother. Ruby says, "Mom, let's eat out! I know a new restaurant. It has delicious noodles." But Ruby's mother does not want to eat out. She wants to stay home. She says, "Ruby, that restaurant's food is not healthy. We can make healthy noodles at home." Ruby is not happy. She says, "Cooking is slow. I want to eat right now. At the restaurant, we can order food. It is fast and easy." Ruby's mother says, "No. Not tonight." Ruby asks, "Then when can I go to that restaurant?" Ruby's mother says, "On your birthday. Now wash your hands."

New Words

noodle

eat out

healthy

order

Part A. Sentence Completion

1. Let's _____ now!

   (A) eat

   (B) to eat

   (C) be eat

   (D) eating

2. _____ can we go there? Tonight? Tomorrow?

   (A) Who

   (B) What

   (C) When

   (D) Where

Part B. Situational Writing

3.  Do you like _____?

   (A) pizza

   (B) salad

   (C) noodles

   (D) hamburgers

4.  We can _____ pizza by phone.

   (A) stay

   (B) heat

   (C) cook

   (D) order

5. What is the most expensive food?

   (A) Chicken

   (B) Fruit Salad

   (C) Cherry Pie

   (D) Tomato Pasta

6. What is NOT on the menu?

   (A) pie

   (B) cake

   (C) juice

   (D) salad

Ruby is hungry. She knows a new restaurant. The restaurant is called "Fat Noodles." Ruby wants to eat at Fat Noodles. She finds her mother. Ruby says, "Mom, let's eat out! I know a new restaurant. It has delicious noodles." But Ruby's mother does not want to eat out. She wants to stay home. She says, "Ruby, that restaurant's food is not healthy. We can make healthy noodles at home." Ruby is not happy. She says, "Cooking is slow. I want to eat right now. At the restaurant, we can order food. It is fast and easy." Ruby's mother says, "No. Not tonight." Ruby asks, "Then when can I go to that restaurant?" Ruby's mother says, "On your birthday. Now wash your hands."

7. What is the best title?

   (A) Home and School
   (B) Ruby Cooks at Home
   (C) Hamburgers or Bread
   (D) Eating Out or Eating at Home

8. What does Ruby like to eat?

   (A) cake
   (B) yogurt
   (C) noodles
   (D) hamburgers

9. Where does Ruby want to go?

   (A) to a birthday party
   (B) to a new restaurant
   (C) to her uncle's house
   (D) to her mother's store

10. Why does Ruby's mother want to eat at home?

   (A) cheap food
   (B) healthy food
   (C) rainy weather
   (D) snowy weather

UNIT 10 Eating Out vs. Eating at Home

Listening Practice

 Listen and write.

  MP3 S2-10

Eating Out vs. Eating at Home

Ruby is hungry. She knows a new restaurant. The restaurant is called "Fat ¹_____ ." Ruby wants to eat at Fat Noodles. She finds her mother. Ruby says, "Mom, let's eat out! I know a new restaurant. It has delicious noodles." But Ruby's mother does not want to ²_____ . She wants to stay home. She says, "Ruby, that restaurant's food is not ³_____ . We can make healthy noodles at home." Ruby is not happy. She says, "Cooking is slow. I want to eat right now. At the restaurant, we can ⁴_____ food. It is fast and easy." Ruby's mother says, "No. Not tonight." Ruby asks, "Then when can I go to that restaurant?" Ruby's mother says, "On your birthday. Now wash your hands."

Word Bank

Nudles	healthy
helthy	eat out
older	eatout
Noodles	order

 Listen. Pause. Say each sentence.

  MP3 S2-10G

Writing Practice

 Write the words.

1

2

3

4

 Write the words.

Summary

Ruby wants to eat at a new restaurant called "Fat Noodles". So she says to
her mother "Let's _____!" But Ruby's mother wants to eat
healthy noodles at home.

M	N	T	X	S	H	D	I	C	U	S	B	G	B	J
G	Y	D	N	C	H	E	A	L	T	H	Y	N	R	E
P	Q	M	Z	Y	G	F	P	W	Q	J	B	U	A	E
U	X	K	Q	U	M	M	E	Q	H	P	Y	Z	C	D
J	M	C	K	Y	I	P	A	Z	B	F	T	G	C	Z
N	P	B	V	Z	C	I	T	J	O	Z	B	H	Z	L
O	W	R	I	U	U	X	O	U	U	P	D	S	M	A
X	K	H	F	B	Z	F	U	R	I	B	A	P	K	Y
E	D	V	S	Y	L	F	T	F	U	C	U	A	O	P
L	B	M	D	V	J	A	K	H	V	U	E	X	R	J
A	O	G	N	M	U	O	R	D	E	R	A	S	A	G
X	A	U	M	A	N	K	X	G	X	C	L	X	W	M
O	I	L	A	Y	G	K	L	W	J	F	X	B	G	F
L	P	V	A	P	H	L	T	I	R	G	F	F	N	T
T	M	N	T	K	N	O	O	D	L	E	F	R	X	E

Write the words. Then find them in the puzzle.

1 _____

2 _____

3 _____

4 _____

UNIT 11

Henry's Family

Teacher's Book
p.141

How many people are in your family?
Can you name them?

Henry lives in a small village. He lives in a very big house. Who lives with Henry? Many people live with Henry. The house has three floors. His grandparents live on the first floor. They grow plants in the garden. They also watch Henry's little cousins. Henry and his parents live on the second floor. They watch movies together at home. Henry's uncle, aunt, and cousins live on the top floor. Henry's cousins are really little. His cousin is only three years old. The other is five years old. They always run in the house. Henry can hear them. His cousins are noisy, but they are cute. Henry likes his life in a big house with his family.

New Words

village

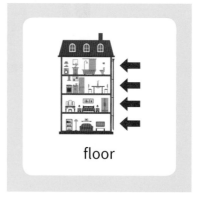

floor

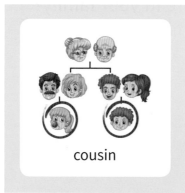

cousin

noisy

Part A. Sentence Completion

1. My grandparents _____ near my school.

   (A) live

   (B) liver

   (C) lives

   (D) living

2. My cousins _____ young children.

   (A) is

   (B) be

   (C) are

   (D) can

Part B. Situational Writing

3.

   This house has _____ floors.

   (A) two

   (B) three

   (C) four

   (D) five

4.

   They are too _____! I cannot sleep.

   (A) tall

   (B) quiet

   (C) short

   (D) noisy

The Finger Family Song

Daddy Finger, Daddy Finger, where are you?
On the paper. On the paper. How do you do?

Mommy Finger, Mommy Finger, where are you?
In your nose. In your nose. How do you do?

Brother Finger, Brother Finger, where are you?
I'm hiding. I'm hiding. How do you do?

Sister Finger, Sister Finger, where are you?
Inside a ring. Inside a ring. How do you do?

Baby Finger, Baby Finger, where are you?
In your ear. In your ear. How do you do?

5. Where is Sister Finger?

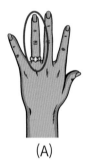

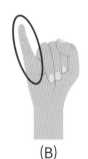

(A) (B) (C) (D)

6. Which finger is hiding?

(A) Baby Finger

(B) Daddy Finger

(C) Brother Finger

(D) Mommy Finger

Part D. General Reading and Retelling

Henry lives in a small village. He lives in a very big house. Who lives with Henry? Many people live with Henry. The house has three floors. His grandparents live on the first floor. They grow plants in the garden. They also watch Henry's little cousins. Henry and his parents live on the second floor. They watch movies together at home. Henry's uncle, aunt, and cousins live on the top floor. Henry's cousins are really little. His cousin is only three years old. The other is five years old. They always run in the house. Henry can hear them. His cousins are noisy, but they are cute. Henry likes his life in a big house with his family.

7. What is the best title?

   (A) Henry Has a Small House
   (B) Henry Live with His Family
   (C) Henry's Cousins are Quiet
   (D) Henry's Parents Go Downtown

8. What is NOT true about Henry's house?

   (A) It is very big.
   (B) It has a garden.
   (C) It is in a large city.
   (D) It has three floors.

9. Where does Henry's aunt live?

   (A) first floor
   (B) second floor
   (C) third floor
   (D) fourth floor

10. Why are Henry's cousins noisy?

   (A) They run.
   (B) They sing.
   (C) They fight.
   (D) They play the piano.

Listening Practice

 Listen and write.

  MP3 S2-11

Henry's Family

Henry lives in a small ¹_____. He lives in a very big house.
Who lives with Henry? Many people live with Henry. The house has three
²_____. His grandparents live on the first floor. They grow
plants in the garden. They also watch Henry's little cousins. Henry and
his parents live on the second floor. They watch movies together at home.
Henry's uncle, aunt, and ³_____ live on the top floor. Henry's
cousins are really little. His cousin is only three years old. The other is five
years old. They always run in the house. Henry can hear them. His cousins
are ⁴_____, but they are cute. Henry likes his life in a big house
with his family.

Word Bank

billage	cousins
flors	niosy
noisy	village
cuzins	floors

 Listen. Pause. Say each sentence.

  MP3 S2-11G

Writing Practice

 Write the words.

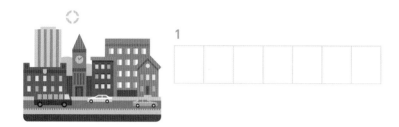

1

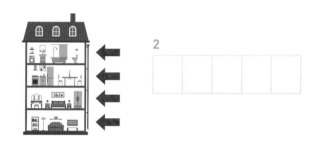

2

3

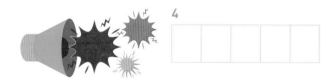

4

 Write the words.

Summary

Henry and his family live in a big house. His grandparents live on the first

_____, Henry and his parents live on the second floor, and

Henry's uncle, aunt, and cousins live on the top floor.

Word Puzzle

X	V	S	C	R	H	D	I	I	A	U	J	J	A	N
W	F	R	A	L	W	C	G	R	P	R	D	V	Z	C
Q	F	K	U	J	F	G	A	E	H	X	I	P	V	S
D	G	K	K	O	V	C	V	I	L	L	A	G	E	G
M	L	T	P	W	Y	F	O	D	M	J	N	I	B	P
P	K	D	J	H	L	O	M	K	E	I	K	S	A	L
V	P	R	G	F	N	Q	I	D	D	P	D	I	N	N
F	C	S	Z	E	C	Z	X	H	F	K	B	R	H	O
G	Q	V	Y	V	T	Y	R	P	H	Z	A	R	Z	I
A	V	L	I	C	G	W	Y	A	I	C	S	D	Q	S
J	N	F	E	J	Q	T	F	R	U	R	S	B	Z	Y
R	S	M	H	V	M	P	L	A	J	M	A	V	Z	A
W	I	C	B	H	R	C	O	U	S	I	N	R	M	G
Q	G	J	V	B	V	I	O	U	Z	P	D	D	D	P
X	Z	J	I	V	U	I	R	I	Y	L	E	Z	I	G

 Write the words. Then find them in the puzzle.

1 _____

2 _____

3 _____

4 _____

UNIT 12

My Aunt's Wedding Day

Teacher's Book p.145

Think! You are at a wedding. Who is there?

My name is Jan. Today is my aunt's wedding day. She is marrying Joe. Who is at the wedding? I see my grandparents. They are wearing beautiful blue clothes. I see my uncles. They are wearing black suits. The wedding starts at one o'clock. We enter the wedding hall. There are many people inside. Joe walks to the front. He is in a shiny black suit. My brother plays the piano. I'm the flower girl. I wear yellow. I put flowers on the floor. My aunt walks to the front. She is wearing a shiny wedding dress. She and Joe look at each other. They say, "I love you." Everyone cries. I cry, too! Every guest stands up. We all clap.

New Words

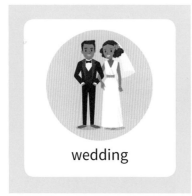

wedding

suit

shiny

clap

Part A. Sentence Completion

1. _____ day is it today?

    (A) Who

    (B) Why

    (C) What

    (D) Where

2. The words _____ beautiful.

    (A) is

    (B) be

    (C) are

    (D) being

Part B. Situational Writing

3.

    The shoe is _____!

    (A) dirty

    (B) shiny

    (C) brown

    (D) square

4.

    He is wearing a black _____ and a blue tie.

    (A) hat

    (B) bag

    (C) suit

    (D) scarf

UNIT 12 My Aunt's Wedding Day

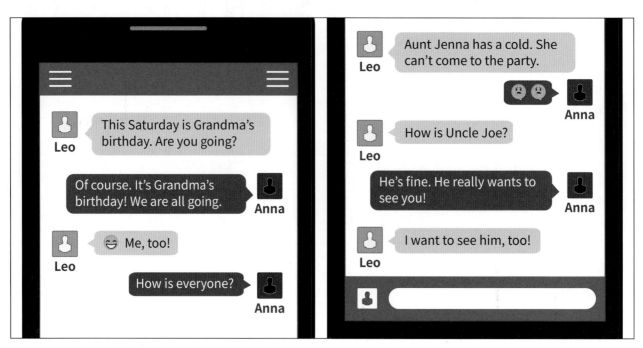

5. When is the party?

(A) Thursday

(B) Friday

(C) Saturday

(D) Sunday

6. Who is NOT going to the party?

(A) Leo

(B) Anna

(C) Uncle Joe

(D) Aunt Jenna

Part D. General Reading and Retelling

My name is Jan. Today is my aunt's wedding day. She is marrying Joe. Who is at the wedding? I see my grandparents. They are wearing beautiful blue clothes. I see my uncles. They are wearing black suits. The wedding starts at one o'clock. We enter the wedding hall. There are many people inside. Joe walks to the front. He is in a shiny black suit. My brother plays the piano. I'm the flower girl. I wear yellow. I put flowers on the floor. My aunt walks to the front. She is wearing a shiny wedding dress. She and Joe look at each other. They say, "I love you." Everyone cries. I cry, too! Every guest stands up. We all clap.

7. What is the best title?

(A) Shiny Wedding Dress

(B) My Aunt's Wedding Day

(C) Beautiful Wedding Rings

(D) Flowers for a Wedding Cake

8. Who is wearing blue clothes?

(A) Joe

(B) Jan

(C) uncles

(D) grandparents

9. What time does the wedding start?

(A) 1:00

(B) 2:00

(C) 3:00

(D) 4:00

10. What does Jan do?

(A) play the piano

(B) say, "I love you"

(C) dance in the hall

(D) put flowers on the floor

Listening Practice

 Listen and write.

  MP3 S2-12

My Aunt's Wedding Day

My name is Jan. Today is my aunt's ___¹___ day. She is marrying Joe. Who is at the wedding? I see my grandparents. They are wearing beautiful blue clothes. I see my uncles. They are wearing black ___²___. The wedding starts at one o'clock. We enter the wedding hall. There are many people inside. Joe walks to the front. He is in a ___³___ black suit. My brother plays the piano. I'm the flower girl. I wear yellow. I put flowers on the floor. My aunt walks to the front. She is wearing a shiny wedding dress. She and Joe look at each other. They say, "I love you." Everyone cries. I cry, too! Every guest stands up. We all ___⁴___.

Word Bank

siny	suts
clap	wedding
suits	weding
shiny	clep

 Listen. Pause. Say each sentence.

  MP3 S2-12G

Writing Practice

 Write the words.

 1

 2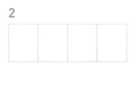

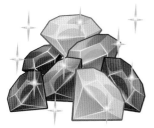 3

 4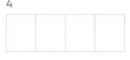

 Write the words.

Summary

Today is my aunt's _____ day. She is marrying Joe. Many people come to the wedding. My aunt and Joe say, "I love you." Everyone cries and claps.

Word Puzzle

S	S	A	D	U	T	Q	B	D	L	Z	O	W	S	H
Q	Y	E	I	U	I	S	P	E	Y	O	V	E	F	X
W	E	D	D	I	N	G	V	C	J	Y	S	Z	E	W
L	N	D	K	G	R	M	M	L	B	W	W	B	V	F
E	G	M	U	W	B	H	E	A	C	J	M	E	H	R
A	B	O	E	S	Y	F	R	P	B	A	X	M	M	E
U	O	T	Q	H	E	B	I	D	S	P	C	U	C	H
O	D	I	N	I	X	U	F	R	K	E	G	L	P	L
Y	J	Y	L	N	X	C	Q	R	Z	U	W	O	L	K
F	R	W	P	Y	Z	E	N	S	N	Y	C	Y	L	Q
H	Z	L	U	Y	V	D	N	U	I	O	V	L	V	C
D	I	C	D	Z	C	R	W	U	S	Z	J	N	Q	I
L	K	D	F	W	Y	A	Q	O	H	K	D	U	C	M
S	U	I	T	D	R	D	O	R	Z	W	K	S	C	K
X	A	U	U	D	Q	P	B	M	X	E	T	J	W	N

Write the words. Then find them in the puzzle.

1 _____ 2 _____ 3 _____ 4 _____

CHAPTER REVIEW

 Match the pictures to the correct words.

candle

carrot

clap

cousin

delicious

eat out

flame

floor

healthy

noisy

noodle

order

shiny

suit

village

wedding

ANSWERS

UNIT 1	⏱	1 (D)	2 (C)	3 (D)	4 (A)	5 (B)	6 (D)	7 (D)	8 (C)	9 (A)	10 (B)
▶ S2-1	🎧	1 downtown		2 action		3 leave		4 arrive			
p.11	✏	1 downtown		2 action movie		3 leave		4 arrive		📄 movie theater	
	✹	1 downtown		2 action movie		3 leave		4 arrive			
UNIT 2	⏱	1 (B)	2 (B)	3 (C)	4 (D)	5 (A)	6 (C)	7 (A)	8 (A)	9 (A)	10 (D)
▶ S2-2	🎧	1 makes		2 washes		3 dressed		4 snack			
p.19	✏	1 make the bed		2 wash your face		3 get dressed		4 make a snack		📄 Every day	
	✹	1 make the bed		2 wash your face		3 get dressed		4 make a snack			
UNIT 3	⏱	1 (A)	2 (A)	3 (D)	4 (A)	5 (C)	6 (D)	7 (D)	8 (A)	9 (D)	10 (B)
▶ S2-3	🎧	1 fresh		2 closet		3 bookshelf		4 mops			
p.27	✏	1 fresh		2 closet		3 bookshelf		4 mop		📄 closet	
	✹	1 fresh		2 closet		3 bookshelf		4 mop			
UNIT 4	⏱	1 (A)	2 (A)	3 (C)	4 (C)	5 (D)	6 (B)	7 (A)	8 (D)	9 (A)	10 (B)
▶ S2-4	🎧	1 pack		2 arrives		3 chimney		4 great			
p.35	✏	1 pack		2 arrive at		3 chimney		4 have a great time		📄 trip	
	✹	1 pack		2 arrive at		3 chimney		4 have a great time			

UNIT 5	⏱	1 (D)	2 (D)	3 (C)	4 (A)	5 (A)	6 (B)	7 (B)	8 (D)	9 (C)	10 (C)
▶ S2-5	🎧	1 country		2 yard		3 windows		4 carpet			
p.45	✏	1 country		2 yard		3 carpet		4 window		📄 dream	
	✹	1 country		2 yard		3 carpet		4 window			
UNIT 6	⏱	1 (A)	2 (C)	3 (D)	4 (C)	5 (A)	6 (C)	7 (B)	8 (A)	9 (C)	10 (B)
▶ S2-6	🎧	1 chairs		2 bookshelf		3 across		4 stove			
p.53	✏	1 chair		2 bookshelf		3 across from		4 stove		📄 chairs	
	✹	1 chair		2 bookshelf		3 across from		4 stove			
UNIT 7	⏱	1 (D)	2 (B)	3 (C)	4 (C)	5 (A)	6 (C)	7 (B)	8 (C)	9 (B)	10 (A)
▶ S2-7	🎧	1 special		2 earphones		3 picture		4 diary			
p.61	✏	1 earphones		2 special		3 picture		4 diary		📄 special	
	✹	1 earphones		2 special		3 picture		4 diary			
UNIT 8	⏱	1 (D)	2 (D)	3 (D)	4 (B)	5 (B)	6 (A)	7 (D)	8 (D)	9 (B)	10 (C)
▶ S2-8	🎧	1 beach		2 forest		3 water		4 inside			
p.69	✏	1 beach		2 forest		3 water park		4 inside		📄 summer vacation	
	✹	1 beach		2 forest		3 water park		4 inside			

UNIT 9	⏱	1 (A)	2 (A)	3 (B)	4 (C)	5 (A)	6 (B)	7 (B)	8 (A)	9 (C)	10 (C)
▶ S2-9	🎧	1 carrot		2 candles		3 flames		4 delicious			
p.79	✏	1 carrot		2 candle		3 flame		4 delicious		📄 candles	
	✹	1 carrot		2 candle		3 flame		4 delicious			
UNIT 10	⏱	1 (A)	2 (C)	3 (C)	4 (D)	5 (D)	6 (B)	7 (D)	8 (C)	9 (B)	10 (B)
▶ S2-10	🎧	1 Noddles		2 eat out		3 healthy		4 order			
p.87	✏	1 noodle		2 eat out		3 healthy		4 order		📄 eat out	
	✹	1 noodle		2 eat out		3 healthy		4 order			
UNIT 11	⏱	1 (A)	2 (C)	3 (B)	4 (D)	5 (A)	6 (C)	7 (B)	8 (C)	9 (C)	10 (A)
▶ S2-11	🎧	1 village		2 floors		3 cousins		4 noisy			
p.95	✏	1 village		2 floor		3 cousin		4 noisy		📄 floor	
	✹	1 village		2 floor		3 cousin		4 noisy			
UNIT 12	⏱	1 (C)	2 (C)	3 (B)	4 (C)	5 (C)	6 (D)	7 (B)	8 (D)	9 (A)	10 (D)
▶ S2-12	🎧	1 wedding		2 suits		3 shiny		4 clap			
p.103	✏	1 wedding		2 suit		3 shiny		4 clap		📄 wedding	
	✹	1 wedding		2 suit		3 shiny		4 clap			